CLINT EASTWOOD

CLINT EASTWOOD
A Life in Pictures

Edited by Pierre-Henri Verlhac
Foreword by Peter Bogdanovich

CHRONICLE BOOKS

SAN FRANCISCO

The Shy Kid from Oakland

By Peter Bogdanovich

Clint Eastwood has had one of the most remarkable careers in the history of the movies. He came into the business just as the original studios' star system was beginning to fall apart around him. As a kind of swan's song, the canny old system plunked young Clint into Westerns as early as 1956, but Westerns were mainly moving over from the big screen to the little one, and so Eastwood became the first great film star to emerge from series television.

Rawhide went on the air in 1959 and ran seven seasons. By the time Clint appeared in his first starring feature, *A Fistful of Dollars*, in 1964, he was already a likeable and popular television star,

a beefcake cowboy with boyish charm. But as the system collapsed in the early 1960s, Eastwood would continue re-creating himself, doing variations on his image, mostly self-directed and -produced—with greater longevity, consistency, and popularity than any other star in pictures. Among others of his ilk, Charlie Chaplin comes first to mind, since he was also famous as a one-man band. But Chaplin's run was just a little over two decades. Clint Eastwood has maintained stardom, largely through his own efforts, for more than forty years.

On top of that, he has been accepted for some time now as one of America's finest directors. And he has been equally noted as one of the most economical: Because of Eastwood's famous speed and efficiency, his films always cost considerably less than what virtually anyone else could have made them for. So he is not only the first movie legend to have been born after the studio system fell apart, but also (along with only Jack Nicholson) the last in the line of the great movie star–actors of old. And he joins an exalted American company of Western heroes: the run goes from Douglas Fairbanks to William S. Hart to Gary Cooper to John Wayne to James Stewart to Clint Eastwood.

During a long, in-depth interview I did with Clint in 2005, he referred to himself without irony as "that shy kid from Oakland." He grew up in California and on the road during the depths of the Depression, learned to play jazz piano beautifully, and always had an innate artistic sensibility. He remained very close to his mother until she died recently in her mid-90s. In person today, Eastwood is still boyish and still very likeable, modest, extremely intelligent, and utterly disarming. Like many musicians, he speaks sometimes with a slightly distracted air, as though hearing a distant tune in his head. And if he is in the self-effacing, laconic, reticent tradition of Gary Cooper, he has certainly known instinctively right from the start what was best for him, and has expressed his will with a steadfast iron hand. As a kid, Clint told me, he never wanted to be an actor. He went on:

> I was too introverted to be an actor. I think now being an introvert helps you sometimes being an actor, because a lot of actors are introverted. They use acting as a way of getting out of themselves. . . . The whole idea of acting is to be in a fantasy—to live something you're not. I think there's something liberating in that. . . . Playing detectives has always been fun to me, I guess because when you're a kid, you do it. As a kid you're always out playing cops and robbers. I think if, as a kid, you see Gary Cooper riding across the plains, you think it would be fun to do that, to be a guy like that or a detective or whatever. Maybe that's what attracts a lot of people to being an actor—you get to play all those things.

But in the performing field, young Clint was mainly into music. He never took piano lessons, but at the age of eleven or twelve, he started bringing records home:

And I'd listen to them and pick out what they were doing and play it on the piano. My mother always thought that was unique. . . . I was kind of a shy kid, and I was at a party one time . . . one guy was playing a boogie tune, and I said, "I can play it better than that." Finally I sat down and played one tune I'd been fooling with at home, and all of a sudden all the girls started coming around the piano . . . so I thought, "This isn't so bad, I'm going home and practice . . ." Then I used to go down to a place called the Omar Club in Oakland, and I played in there. I was about sixteen by that time, and they'd give me pizza and a beer . . . I played a lot as a kid. I used to play at gin mills all around Oakland—wherever I could get a free pizza or something.

When the Korean War came along, Eastwood had tried to enroll in Seattle University because of their excellent music department, but the army had other plans, and he was drafted. Out after two years, he enrolled at L.A. City College, majoring in business administration. "But I started going to acting classes at night with a few friends. I just kind of started getting interested in it. I didn't participate, but I was watching."

Then, through a series of coincidences, he eventually did a screen test at Universal Studios and got a contract at about $75 a week. (Before that, he had been working at a Signal Oil gas station.) After numerous bit parts on TV and in B-movies, he eventually landed *Rawhide*, mainly because he was a good rider, having ridden horses from the time he was a kid. His parents were good riders. He told me, "When I got into the acting thing it actually was the first discipline I've ever been able to say, 'Okay, if I'm going to do this, I've got to really do this. I can't screw around, I can't fake my way along.' So I think that in the '50s I grew up—late."

Even back then, he wanted to direct, but when he asked if he could do an episode, he was turned down. I questioned what had made him want to direct:

I was just always curious about it. I liked the photographing of the story, the bringing-scenes-to-life aspect of it. . . . I always liked the idea. I like the arranging of it all—the casting of it all—the breathing life into it, seeing it come alive—coming alive from just a book or screenplay or what have you. Having it come alive before you and one day you look at it and say, "There it is, it's a screenplay that's all done." It's a feeling you never lose—the excitement about it. As a young actor, you never see it as something within your grasp.

When the offer came to star in a low-budget spaghetti Western, made under particularly primitive conditions, Eastwood's sense of adventure led him to accept. He was also sophisticated enough to know that the Italian script was a clever rip-off of a distinguished Samurai film of Akira Kurosawa's (*Yojimbo*, 1961). And, observing that the director, Sergio Leone, had a distinctly operatic bent, his approach was to play radically against it. "I just played him as grimy and grumpy as I knew how at that age of mine," Eastwood told me in his understated way. "After you work with Sergio you realize he's doing things slightly operatic. So I played in the opposite direction—and it seemed to work out. I figured if I got operatic, then we'd do it too broad. . . . So if Sergio was playing it slightly broad, I was playing it slightly the other way and trying to balance it out."

Indeed, Eastwood's brilliant choice gives the three Leone pictures (the other two are *For a Few Dollars More*, 1965, and *The Good, the Bad and the*

Ugly, 1966) a fascinating tension that propelled them to huge grosses and turned Eastwood into an international superstar. Within two years, he was working with the veteran American director who most influenced Clint's work as a filmmaker, Don Siegel. A tough, hard-hitting, no-nonsense, sophisticated yet unpretentious director, Siegel had made a number of tightly-structured low-budget classics such as *Riot in Cell Block 11* (1955) and the original *Invasion of the Body Snatchers* (1956). In 1968, Siegel and Eastwood did their first of five pictures together, *Coogan's Bluff*, which cleverly moved Eastwood from the old West into the modern day by casting him as a contemporary Western sheriff come to New York to track down a criminal.

Three years later, after two period Siegel pictures (*Two Mules for Sister Sara*, 1970, and *The Beguiled*, 1971), came their breakthrough film, *Dirty Harry*, which finally and for all time established Eastwood's enduring non-Western persona. I interviewed Siegel around the time he was finishing *Coogan's Bluff* and he told me candidly:

> Clint Eastwood has an absolute fixation on the antihero. It's his credo in life and in all the films that he's done so far. And it has

been very successful, certainly for Clint Eastwood and for those who own a piece of his pictures. He insists on being an antihero. I've never worked with an actor who was less concerned with his good image. Where you would tread very lightly on certain suggestions to another actor—like, Why don't you have an affair and make the girl seventeen years of age?—he insists on that.

When I repeated this to Clint, he said, laughing, "I don't know about the 'seventeen years of age'! That would get me in trouble." He continued, "But, yeah, whenever we would do something that was really unheroic by movie-protagonist standards, I just jump right in." He thought maybe he had been most influenced by his favorite actor, James Cagney, in Raoul Walsh's *White Heat* (1949), eating a chicken leg as he shoots a man to death through the trunk of a car. Eastwood explained to me, "I kind of decided that I was gonna say, 'Hey, the audience is gonna go with me or not, and if they don't like it, it's too bad.'"

At the first industry screening of *Dirty Harry*, I remember Siegel being worried about the picture's impact. He thought all his liberal friends would disown him because of the film's persuasive portrayal of how difficult it has become for police to apprehend criminals. He also told me that Harry's disgusted throwing away of his badge at the end was Eastwood's idea. Clint's attitude to this landmark in his career is revealing of his approach:

When we were making it, not one word of politics was ever spoken—it was never thought of as a political thing—we just thought of it as an exciting detective story, and the fact that the character goes outside the law to get the job done just seemed to me pragmatic. It wasn't like he was a red-state, blue-state guy or whatever. He was a kind of a guy who said, "Hey, I gotta get the job done, I don't give a crap if the law's in the way." And at that particular time in history I think this was appealing to people because everybody was probably getting tired of hearing about "the Miranda" and rights of the accused. It was about time to hear the rights of the victims. So I think it became popular on that level.

That same year, 1971, saw the release of Eastwood's first film as a director, *Play Misty for Me*, a modest, well-crafted suspense story. Over the next thirty-six years, Clint directed another twenty-six pictures, appearing in at least one film a year, often two. He played Inspector "Dirty" Harry Callahan another four times (*Magnum Force*, 1973, *The Enforcer*, 1976, *Sudden Impact*, 1983, *The Dead Pool*, 1988), and directed and starred in the most notable Westerns of the modern era. Indeed, he has been responsible for keeping the genre alive with *High Plains Drifter* (1973), *The Outlaw Josey Wales* (1976), *Pale Rider* (1985), and, what is generally considered to be his masterpiece, *Unforgiven* (1992), which won Oscars for Best Director and Best Picture. Twelve years later, he would repeat this double-win with his starkly offbeat boxing drama *Million Dollar Baby* (2004). Because of these two films, he also remains the only person in Oscar history to have been nominated for both Best Actor and Best Director for the same movie.

Throughout those nearly four decades, Eastwood's pictures (as actor and filmmaker) have largely fallen within established genres, reflecting the kind of filmmaking he most admires and enjoys: Crime/suspense pictures like *Thunderbolt and Lightfoot* (1974), *The Gauntlet* (1977), *In the Line of Fire* (1993), *True Crime* (1999); or war films like *The Eiger*

Sanction (1975), *Firefox* (1982), *Heartbreak Ridge* (1986), and his amazing 2006 double-feature, *Flags of Our Fathers* and *Letters from Iwo Jima*.

However, he has consistently stretched himself with unorthodox, eccentric, untypical, risky, and personal pictures that are often surprising, such as the Depression drama *Honkytonk Man* (1982), the Charlie Parker biopic *Bird* (1988), the African drama with Eastwood as a fictionalized John Huston in *White Hunter, Black Heart* (1990), the complicated social study adapted from the best-seller *Midnight in the Garden of Good and Evil* (1997), and the searing Boston tragedy *Mystic River* (2003). He summed up his personal credo to me succinctly, "You don't make 'em trying to be a success, you just make 'em trying to be the best you can. I think you have to kind of believe in the story and tell the story the best you can. And if it finds an audience, great—if it doesn't, c'est la vie."

Perhaps the most unexpected film of his career and one that proves the extent of his versatility, self-awareness, and depth, was his adaptation of the best-selling romance *The Bridges of Madison County*, released in 1995. As the photographer Robert Kincaid, he gives maybe his most tender and personable performance, and as director, he elicits a beautifully honest and touching portrayal from Meryl Streep, among her finest. Often he would use takes in which she made mistakes in the dialogue because he found them more spontaneous. The scenes between the two of them—often played in long, uninterrupted shots—are absolutely riveting, filled with emotion and the kind of sensitivity Eastwood has shown most frequently in the music he has occasionally composed for movies.

Just when you think you have Eastwood pegged, he will surprise you. In the characters he has played and the films he has made, there is always ambiguity and there are never easy answers. This makes him a modern artist, though his style is essentially classical. He has been honored around the world, and I asked him how he feels about all that celebration of his achievements. He characterized it modestly as "pretty nice."

> Sometimes somebody runs a series of film clips, like the AFI or Lincoln Center or whatever, you kind of go, "Yeah, Jesus, I did a lot of stuff, didn't I? How about that?" But you don't think about it, because you're going on to the next thing . . . I guess if the person can just look back and say, "You know, I did a few good films and had a good career. I didn't hurt anybody along the way. What the hell, I didn't trip too hard over myself." That's kind of a good thing to be able to say, I guess. I don't know what else you can ask for beyond that.

And with that, he was off to the next thing.

A young Clint Eastwood in the 1950s.

Above:
1954 | San Francisco, CA | Actresses Olive Sturgess (left) and Dani Crayne (right) flank Clint Eastwood.

Opposite:
1956 | Clint Eastwood was a promising young actor in Arthur Lubin's *The First Traveling Saleslady*, with Ginger Rogers, Barry Nelson, Carol Channing, David Brian, and James Arness.

Pages 16–17:
1955 | Clint Eastwood and his classmates (from left) Jane Howard, Myrna Hansen, and Dani Crane.

"My family was too busy moving around, looking for work, for me to know what I wanted. Even after I got out of high school, I had no idea what I wanted to do."

Clint Eastwood

Above and opposite:
1956 | Clint Eastwood and Carol Channing in *The First Traveling Saleslady*, directed by Arthur Lubin.

1955 | Portrait.

May 30, 1959 | Santa Monica, CA | Clint Eastwood and his wife, Maggie Johnson, enjoying the Union 76 Ocean Highway section of Pacific Ocean Park, an amusement park in Santa Monica.

Left and opposite:
1959 | Clint Eastwood playing the
role of Rowdy Yates in the television
series *Rawhide*, directed by Jus Addis.
Eastwood acted in 217 episodes between
1959 and 1965.

"We called him 'mumbles.' He didn't speak his words very loud. The soundman was always saying, 'Kid, speak up!' But he mumbled his way to a fortune."

Sheb Wooley

October 1959 | Clint Eastwood listening to music at home.

Above:
1960 | Clint Eastwood at home with his 1958 Jaguar XK 150.

Opposite:
1961 | Clint Eastwood and his wife, Maggie.

Left and opposite:
1961 | Sherman Oaks, CA |
Outdoor portraits of
Clint Eastwood.

Above:
October 25, 1962 | Clint Eastwood with his wife, Maggie, in the pool at their home in Hollywood Hills.

Opposite:
September 17, 1964 | Las Vegas, NV | Clint Eastwood at the Sahara Hotel.

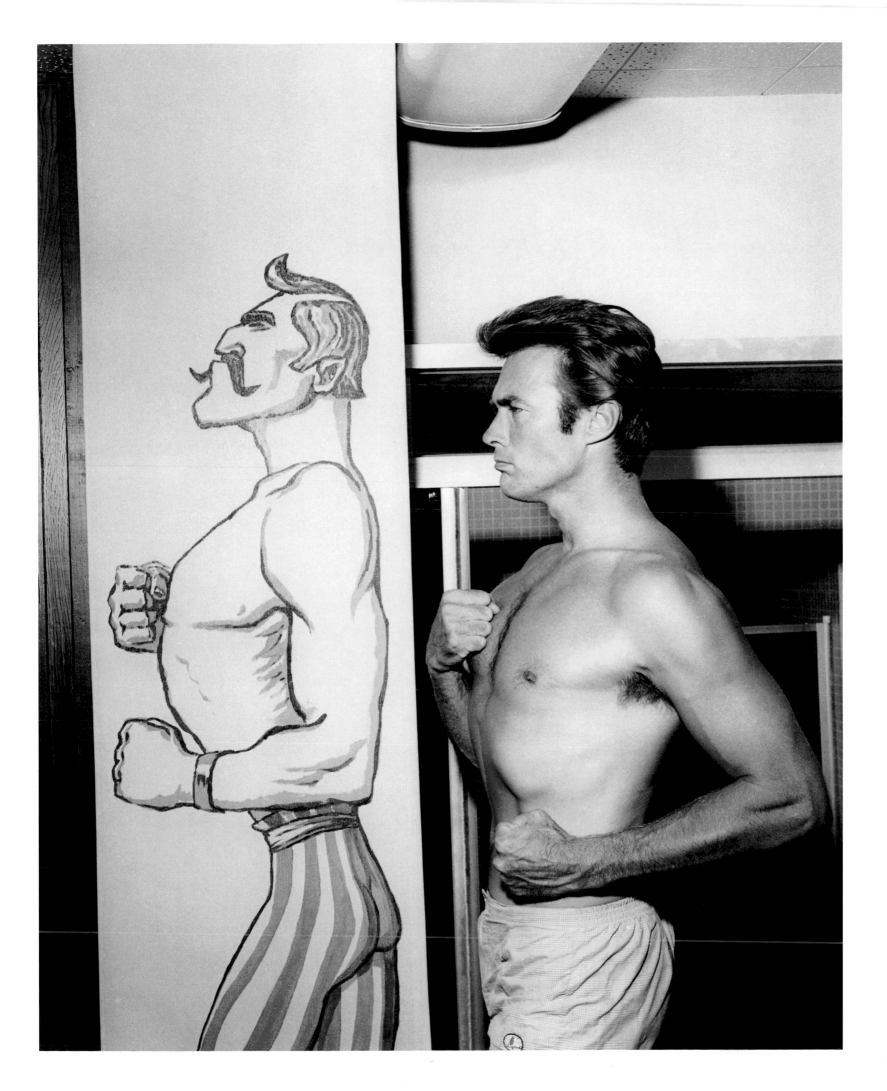

"I like people who stand up for their ideas without relenting. The day I told my father that I was going to study drama, he told me 'Don't do that. Get a real job.'"

Clint Eastwood, interview with *L'Express* magazine, 2006

Opposite:
September 22, 1964 | Portrait.

1960s | Clint Eastwood at home.

1965 | Clint Eastwood with his Ferrari 275 GTB.

Left and opposite:
1965 | Hollywood Hills, CA | Clint
Eastwood at home.

Left:
1964 | Italy | Clint Eastwood in Sergio Leone's *A Fistful of Dollars.*

Opposite:
A 1966 portrait.

1965 | Italy | Clint Eastwood in Sergio Leone's *For a Few Dollars More.*

For Three Men The Civil War Wasn't Hell. It Was Practice!

CLINT EASTWOOD in

"THE GOOD, THE BAD and THE UGLY"

co-starring
LEE VAN CLEEF

ALDO GIUFFRE | and with MARIO BREGA

also starring
ELI WALLACH
in the role of Tuco

SERGIO LEONE

Screenplay by AGE-SCARPELLI, LUCIANO VINCENZONI and SERGIO LEONE   Directed by SERGIO LEONE   Music by ENNIO MORRICONE
Produced by ALBERTO GRIMALDI FOR P.E.A.—Produzioni Europee Associate, Rome

TECHNISCOPE® TECHNICOLOR®

Opposite and left: 1964 | Italy | Lee Van Cleef and Clint Eastwood in *The Good, the Bad and the Ugly*, directed by Sergio Leone.

Left and opposite:
1968 | Clint Eastwood playing sheriff
Walt Coogan opposite Susan Clark in
Coogan's Bluff, directed by Don Siegel.

Left:
1968 | Baker, OR | Clint Eastwood
on the set of the film *Paint Your
Wagon*, directed by Joshua Logan.

Opposite:
1967 | Portrait.

"I don't believe in pessimism. If something doesn't come up the way you want, forge ahead. If you think it's going to rain, it will."

Clint Eastwood

1968 | Clint Eastwood as the sheriff in *Coogan's Bluff*.

1969 | Clint Eastwood during the filming of *Two Mules for Sister Sara*, directed by Don Siegel.

1969 | On the set of *Two Mules for Sister Sara*; from left, Shirley MacLaine, Clint Eastwood, and director Don Siegel.

Above:
1969 | Director Don Siegel in conversation with Clint Eastwood on the set of *Two Mules for Sister Sara*.

Pages 58–59:
1969 | John Wayne cutting the cake celebrating his fortieth anniversary in the Hollywood film industry.
From left, Lee Marvin, Clint Eastwood, Rock Hudson, Fred MacMurray, James Stewart, Ernest Borgnine, Michael Caine, and Laurence Harvey.

1970 | Los Angeles, CA | At the Beverly Hilton on the occasion of the 42nd Academy Awards ceremony.

June 1971 | Los Angeles, CA | Clint Eastwood and his wife, Maggie, attending a party in honor of Frank Sinatra, who had officially retired from his film career a few days earlier.

1970 | Irene Hervey and Clint Eastwood in *Play Misty for Me.*

1971 | Clint Eastwood (right) playing Dave Garver in *Play Misty for Me*, which he also directed. Also pictured is Don Siegel, the director of many of Eastwood's other films, playing a bartender named Murphy.

"**When I directed *Play Misty for Me,* no one took me seriously. For the studio, it was sort of 'Let him play with his pocket money, he'll come back for the serious stuff.'**"

Clint Eastwood

1971 | Clint Eastwood on the set of his film
Play Misty for Me.

1971 | Clint Eastwood playing the role of
Captain John McBurney in Don Siegel's
The Beguiled.

1971 | Clint Eastwood on the set of Don Siegel's *The Beguiled.*

Above and opposite:
1971 | Clint Eastwood during the filming of Don Siegel's *The Beguiled.*

Opposite, above, and pages 72–75:
1971 | Clint Eastwood in Don Siegel's *Dirty Harry*.

Above:
1971 | Clint Eastwood during the filming of his self-directed *Play Misty for Me*.

Opposite:
1971 | Clint Eastwood and Jessica Walter in *Play Misty for Me*.

"Few directors exude the same radiant joy that Clint can. His simplicity, his refusal of the luxury of his childhood, and his sincerity contribute enormously to the power of his films."

Tom Stern, ASC, director of photography, talking about his work with Clint Eastwood

Opposite:
1972 | Clint Eastwood playing with his son, Kyle, between takes.

78

Left and opposite:
1972 | Clint Eastwood acting in *Joe Kidd*,
directed by John Sturges.

"Clint permanently surprises me with his vitality and his enthusiasm."

Tom Stern, ASC, director of photography, talking about his work with Clint Eastwood

Pages 82 and 83:
1973 | Clint Eastwood in *Magnum Force*, directed by Ted Post.

84

1973 | Clint Eastwood during the premiere of Richard Sarafian's *The Man who Loved Cat Dancing*.

Above and opposite:
1973 | Clint Eastwood in Ted Post's *Magnum Force*.

Pages 88 and 89:
1973 | Director Clint Eastwood and William Holden discuss camera positions just before filming *Breezy*.

Above and opposite:
1976 | Clint Eastwood playing Josey Wales in *The Outlaw Josey Wales*, which he also directed.

May 24, 1975 | Clint Eastwood discusses a scene with cinematographer Bruce Surtees during the filming of *High Plains Drifter*.

1977 | Clint Eastwood on the set of James Fargo's *The Enforcer*.

Left:
1975 | Clint Eastwood both acted in and directed
The Eiger Sanction.

Opposite:
1975 | Clint Eastwood consulting with actor
George Kennedy on the set of *The Eiger Sanction.*

October 27, 1977 | Clint Eastwood and Sondra Locke on the set of Eastwood's *The Gauntlet*.

1977 | Clint Eastwood and Sondra Locke in *The Gauntlet*.

Above and opposite:
1977 | Clint Eastwood on the set of *The Gauntlet*.

1978 | James Fargo, director of *Every Which Way but Loose* (left), Clint Eastwood, and his colleague, the orangutan Clyde, on the set.

1978 | From left, Beverly D'Angelo, Geoffrey Lewis, the orangutan Clyde, and Clint Eastwood, all actors in James Fargo's *Every Which Way but Loose*.

"There's a rebel lying deep in my soul. Anytime anybody tells me the trend is such and such, I go the opposite direction."

Clint Eastwood

1979 | A still from the Don Siegel film *Escape from Alcatraz*, featuring Clint Eastwood.

An undated portrait of actor, director, and producer Clint Eastwood.

October 1981 | Los Angeles, CA |
Clint Eastwood on the set of his film
Firefox.

1980 | Clint Eastwood playing Bronco Billy McCoy in *Bronco Billy*, which he also directed.

Above:
1980 | Producer Fritz Manes and Clint Eastwood, who played the role of Philo Beddoe in Buddy Van Horn's *Any Which Way You Can*.

Pages 108–111:
October 1981 | Los Angeles, CA | Clint Eastwood on the set of his film *Firefox*.

August 21, 1984 | Hollywood, CA | Clint Eastwood writing his name in the wet cement in front of Mann's Chinese Theatre. He also left his handprint and the phrase, "You made my day." Malpaso (written on his shirt) is the name of his production company.

113

1985 | Clint Eastwood attending the Cannes Film Festival
to present his latest film, *Pale Rider*.

1985 | Paris, France | Clint Eastwood relaxing at Maxim's.

1985 | Portrait of Clint Eastwood at the premiere of *Pale Rider*.

Opposite and above:
1985 | Clint Eastwood during the shooting of his film *Pale Rider*.

April 9, 1986 | Carmel, CA | Following his election as mayor of the city of Carmel, Clint Eastwood proudly displays a T-shirt proclaiming his victory.

April 9, 1986 | Carmel, CA | Clint Eastwood holding a press conference after being elected mayor of the city of Carmel. His victory made headlines in the press.

"What makes him think a middle-aged actor [Clint Eastwood], who's played with a chimp, could have a future in politics?"

Ronald Reagan

MAYOR EASTWOOD

May 6, 1986 | Mayor Clint Eastwood at his
first city council meeting.

Left and opposite:
March 1986 | Clint Eastwood
during the election campaign.

Eastwood earned 72% of the vote, becoming Carmel mayor in 1986.

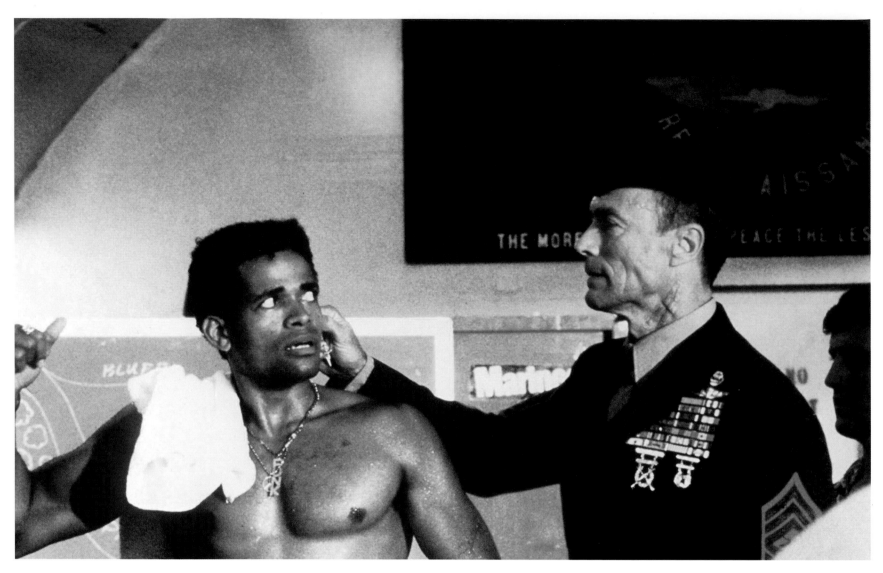

Above and opposite:
1986 | Clint Eastwood played a role in the film *Heartbreak Ridge* as well as directing it.

"I was single when I was mayor of Carmel, but I was so busy doing stuff that I never had time to go out. At about a year and a half I said, 'I might go back and make some more movies.'"

Clint Eastwood, interview with Tony Macklin

1992 | Portrait.

Left and opposite:
1990 | Clint Eastwood acted in and directed the 1990 film *White Hunter, Black Heart*. In the same year, the film was an official selection at the Cannes Film Festival.

"When I did *Unforgiven* I thought it would be the perfect last western for me. It's turned out there's never been a story come along in my career to equal that in that particular genre. So, it may be the last one."

Clint Eastwood, interview with Tony Macklin

1992 | Clint Eastwood, actor in and director of *Unforgiven*. Eastwood was emerging from a period of uncertainty marked by the successive box office failures of films such as *The Rookie* and *White Hunter, Black Heart*. Warner Bros. would not risk producing *Unforgiven*. That was not a wise move on the part of Warner Bros., as *Unforgiven* turned out to be a great success, and relaunched Eastwood's career.

1992 | Carmel, CA | Clint Eastwood at his ranch.

1992 | Clint Eastwood on the set of *Unforgiven*.

1993 | Kevin Costner and Clint Eastwood during the filming of *A Perfect World*, directed by Eastwood.

1993 | Clint Eastwood on the set of *In the Line of Fire*, directed by Wolfgang Petersen.

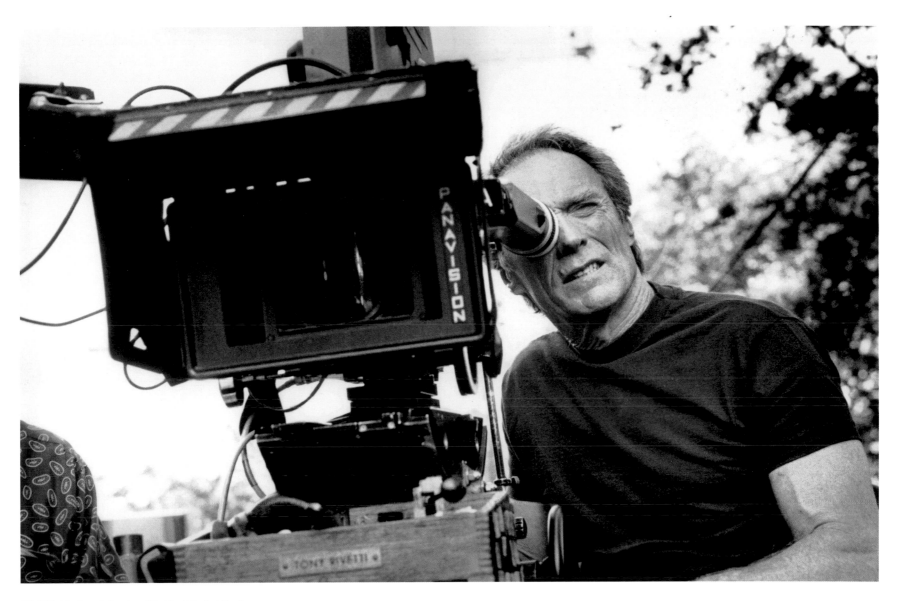

1993 | Clint Eastwood, director of the film *A Perfect World*.

May 12, 1994 | Cannes, France | Catherine Deneuve (right), Clint Eastwood, and his former wife, Maggie (left), arriving at the Palais des Festivals. In that year, Deneuve and Eastwood were co-presidents of the jury of the Cannes Film Festival.

"Of all the characters Clint has portrayed, he most closely resembles that of Robert Kincaid, the free-spirited photographer from *The Bridges of Madison County*."

Dina Ruiz

May 12, 1994 | Cannes, France |
Catherine Deneuve and Clint Eastwood,
co-presidents of the jury of the
Cannes Film Festival.

March 27, 1995 | Los Angeles, CA | Clint Eastwood receiving
the Irving G. Thalberg Memorial Award in the Shrine Auditorium
during the 67th Academy Award ceremonies. This prize is
awarded sporadically to movie producers whose work consistently reflects a high standard of creativity.

Right and pages 148 and 149:
1995 | Meryl Streep and
Clint Eastwood during the
filming of *The Bridges of
Madison County.*

"The blues has always been part of my musical life and the piano has a special place. Also, the music has always played a part in my movies."

Clint Eastwood

Opposite:
October 17, 1996 | New York, NY | Clint Eastwood plays piano on the stage at Carnegie Hall, accompanied by pianist Barry Harris (left) and drummer T. S. Monk Jr. (center). This special jazz event, entitled "Eastwood: After Hours, A Night of Jazz," paid hommage to Clint Eastwood's love for jazz music, which played a major part in most of his films.

150

Above:
1997 | Clint Eastwood shooting *Absolute Power*, in which he also played a role.

Opposite:
March 1996 | Los Angeles, CA | A wedding photo of Clint Eastwood and journalist and anchorwoman Dina Ruiz.

July 22, 1997 | Carmel, CA | In front of his restaurant, Mission Ranch, Clint Eastwood presents a six-pack of Pale Rider Ale, named for his 1985 film *Pale Rider*. Profits from the sale of this ale are donated to charity.

Carmel, CA | Mission Ranch, the restaurant and resort owned by Clint Eastwood.

Left:
February 26, 1998 | Paris, France | Clint Eastwood promoting the film he just directed, *Midnight in the Garden of Good and Evil.*

February 26, 1998 | Paris, France | Clint Eastwood promoting his latest film, *Midnight in the Garden of Good and Evil.*

1999 | Clint Eastwood, producer, director, and actor in *True Crime*, in conversation with James Woods.

"Most people who will remember me, if at all, will remember me as an action guy, which is okay. But there will be a certain group that will remember me for the other films, the ones where I took a few chances. At least, I like to think so."

Clint Eastwood

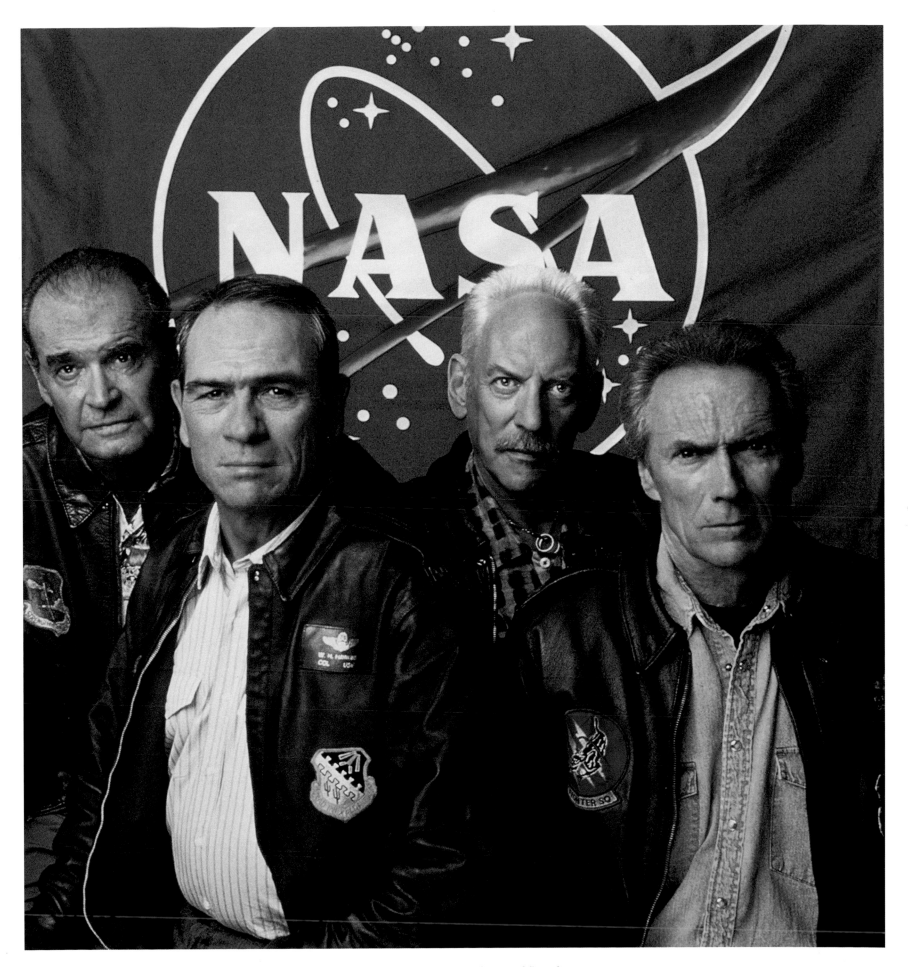

2000 | James Garner, Tommy Lee Jones, Donald Sutherland, and Clint Eastwood on the poster for *Space Cowboys*, which Eastwood directed.

August 1, 2000 | NASA astronaut Yvonne Cagle (left) and researcher Kathryn Clark (center), technical advisors for the filming of *Space Cowboys*, with Clint Eastwood at the premiere of the film.

Above:
2000 | On the set of *Space Cowboys*.

Pages 164 and 165:
2002 | Wrinkled portraits.

Opposite and left:
May 23, 2003 | Cannes, France |
Eastwood presented *Mystic River* at
the 56th Cannes Film Festival. The
film was nominated for six Academy
Awards and received two Oscars
in 2004.

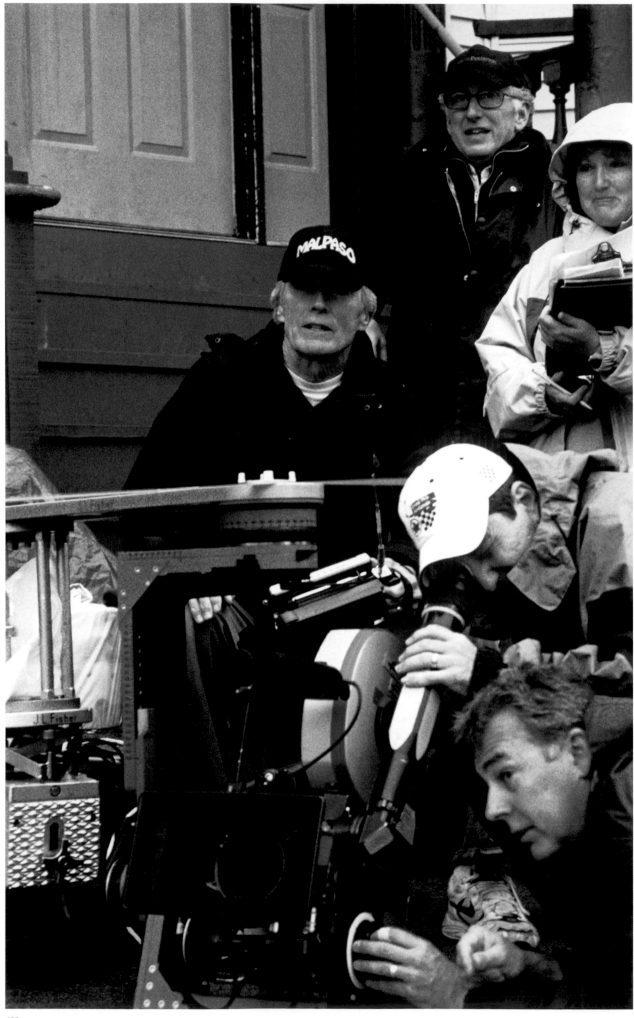

Opposite and above:
2003 | Clint Eastwood on the set of *Mystic River*.

"In *Mystic River,* I didn't act in the picture. It was a great pleasure to shoot with all the younger players, and I thought, 'Yeah, I'm happy back here,' behind the camera."

Clint Eastwood, interview with Tony Macklin

February 22, 2004 | Los Angeles, CA | Sean Penn and Clint Eastwood on the occasion of the 10th awards ceremony of the Screen Actors Guild. Penn was nominated for his role in *Mystic River*.

2004 | Clint Eastwood and Morgan Freeman during the filming of *Million Dollar Baby*, a film Eastwood directed.

2004 | Clint Eastwood and Hilary Swank on the set of *Million Dollar Baby*.

2004 | Clint Eastwood on the set of *Million Dollar Baby*.

January 16, 2005 | Clint Eastwood being awarded the Golden Globe for Best Director for *Million Dollar Baby*.

Opposite and left:
February 27, 2005 | Hollywood, CA |
Clint Eastwood embraces Hilary Swank
as he receives the Best Film Oscar for
Million Dollar Baby.

Pages 178-179:
February 4, 2005 | Hollywood, CA |
In preparation for the 11th annual
Screen Actors Guild Awards, for which
Clint Eastwood and Hilary Swank were
nominated.

"I've always associated myself with films I believe in. I've made some that don't excite me. Today, I'm going to fight for projects that I take seriously, like *Mystic River* and *Million Dollar Baby*, which no one else wanted to do."

Clint Eastwood, interview with *L'Express* magazine, 2006

February 27, 2005 | Hollywood, CA | Clint Eastwood displaying the two Oscars he has just won for his film *Million Dollar Baby*: Best Film and Best Director. Morgan Freeman and Hilary Swank also won Oscars for Best Supporting Actor and Best Actress, respectively.

硫黄島からの Letters from Iwo Jima

November 16, 2006 | Tokyo, Japan | Clint Eastwood appearing beside Ken Watanabe at a press conference about his upcoming film, *Letters from Iwo Jima*.

Above:
December 6, 2006 | Sacramento, CA | During an official ceremony, California governor Arnold Schwarzenegger congratulates Clint Eastwood for being inducted into the California Hall of Fame in 2006. The eleven other honorees were Alice Walker, Amelia Earhart, Billie Jean King, César Chávez, David Ho, Frank Gehry, the Hearst Family, the Packard Family, Ronald Reagan, Sally Ride, and Walt Disney.

Pages 184–185:
January 9, 2007 | New York | Clint Eastwood briefly addresses the press during a gala evening event.

Above:
January 12, 2007 | Santa Monica, CA | Clint Eastwood and producer Steven Spielberg accepting the prize for Best Foreign Language Film for *Letters from Iwo Jima* at the the 12th annual Broadcast Film Critics Association award ceremony.

Opposite:
January 12, 2007 | Santa Monica, CA | Clint Eastwood during the 12th annual Broadcast Film Critics Association award ceremony.

February 5, 2007 | Los Angeles, CA | Sid Gains, president of the Academy of Motion Picture Arts and Sciences, and Clint Eastwood, nominated for the Oscar for Best Director for *Letters from Iwo Jima*, during a dinner for nominees held a few days before the 79th annual Academy Awards ceremonies.

May 11, 2007 | Los Angeles, CA | Clint Eastwood on the campus of the University of Southern California receiving an honorary doctorate for his contribution to cinematic excellence and for the humanism that pervades his films.

FILMOGRAPHY

Year	Title	Director	Character	Additional Credits
1955	*Tarantula*	Jack Arnold	Jet squadron leader	–
1955	*Francis in the Navy*	Arthur Lubin	Jonesey	–
1955	*Lady Godiva (also Lady Godiva of Coventry)*	Arthur Lubin	First Saxon	–
1955	*Revenge of the Creature*	Jack Arnold	Lab assistant	–
1956	*The First Traveling Sales Lady*	Arthur Lubin	Lieutenant Jack Rice	–
1956	*Star in the Dust*	Charles F. Haas	Tom	–
1956	*Never Say Goodbye*	Jerry Hopper	Will	–
1957	*Escapade in Japan*	Arthur Lubin	Dumbo Pilot	–
1958	*Lafayette Escadrille (also With You in My Arms)*	William Wellman	George Moseley	–
1958	*Ambush at Cimarron Pass*	Jodie Copelan	Keith Williams	–
1964	*A Fistful of Dollars*	Sergio Leone	Man with No Name	–
1966	*For a Few Dollars More*	Sergio Leone	Man with No Name	–
1966	*The Witches*	Pier Paolo Pasolini	Mario, Valeria's husband	–
1966	*The Good, the Bad and the Ugly*	Sergio Leone	Man with No Name	–
1968	*Coogan's Bluff*	Don Siegel	Coogan	–
1968	*Hang 'Em High*	Ted Post	Marshal Jed Cooper	–
1969	*Where Eagles Dare*	Brian G. Hutton	Morris Schaffer	–
1969	*Paint Your Wagon*	Joshua Logan	Pardner	–
1970	*Two Mules for Sister Sarah*	Don Siegel	Hogan	–
1970	*Kelly's Heroes*	Brian G. Hutton	Kelly	–
1971	*The Beguiled*	Don Siegel	John McBurney	–
1971	*Play Misty for Me*	Clint Eastwood	Dave Garver	–
1971	*Dirty Harry*	Don Siegel	Inspector Harry Callahan	–
1972	*Joe Kidd*	John Sturges	Joe Kidd	–
1973	*High Plains Drifter*	Clint Eastwood	The Stranger	–
1973	*Magnum Force*	Ted Post	Inspector Harry Callahan	–
1973	*Breezy*	Clint Eastwood	A man in the crowd on the jetty	–
1974	*Thunderbolt and Lightfoot*	Michael Cimino	John "Thunderbolt" Doherty	–
1975	*The Eiger Sanction*	Clint Eastwood	Dr. Jonathan Hemlock	–
1976	*The Outlaw Josey Wales*	Clint Eastwood	Josey Wales	–
1976	*The Enforcer*	James Fargo	Inspector Harry Callahan	–
1977	*The Gauntlet*	Clint Eastwood	Ben Shockley	–
1978	*Every Which Way But Loose*	James Fargo	Philo Beddoe	–
1979	*Escape from Alcatraz*	Don Siegel	Frank Morris	–
1980	*Bronco Billy*	Clint Eastwood	Bronco Billy McCoy	–
1980	*Any Which Way You Can*	Buddy Van Horn	Philo Beddoe	–

FILMOGRAPHY CONT'D

Year	Title	Director	Character	Additional Credits
1982	*Firefox*	Clint Eastwood	Mitchell Gant	Producer
1982	*Honkytonk Man*	Clint Eastwood	Red Stovall	Producer
1983	*Sudden Impact*	Clint Eastwood	Inspector Harry Callahan	Producer
1984	*City Heat*	Richard Benjamin	Lieutenant Speer	–
1984	*Tightrope*	Richard Tuggle	Wes Block	Producer
1985	*Pale Rider*	Clint Eastwood	Preacher	Producer
1986	*Heartbreak Ridge*	Clint Eastwood	Tom Highway	Producer
1988	*Thelonious Monk: Straight, No Chaser*	Charlotte Zwerin	–	Executive producer
1988	*Bird*	Clint Eastwood	–	Producer
1988	*The Dead Pool*	Buddy Van Horn	Inspector Harry Callahan	–
1989	*Pink Cadillac*	Buddy Van Horn	Tommy Nowak	–
1990	*White Hunter, Black Heart*	Clint Eastwood	John Wilson	Producer
1990	*The Rookie*	Clint Eastwood	Nick Pulovski	–
1992	*Unforgiven*	Clint Eastwood	William Munny	Producer, composer
1993	*In the Line of Fire*	Wolfgang Petersen	Secret agent Frank Horrigan	–
1993	*A Perfect World*	Clint Eastwood	Red Garnett	Producer
1994	*A Century of Cinema*	Caroline Thomas	Himself	–
1994	*Don't Pave Main Street: Carmel's Heritage*	William T. Cartwright / Julian Ludwig	–	Narrator
1995	*The Bridges of Madison County*	Clint Eastwood	Robert Kincaid	Producer, composer
1995	*Casper*	Brad Silberling	Cameo audio role	–
1995	*A Personal Journey with Martin Scorsese Through American Movies*	Martin Scorsese	Himself	–
1995	*The Stars Fell on Henrietta*	James Keach	–	Producer
1997	*Absolute Power*	Clint Eastwood	Luther Whitney	Producer, composer
1997	*Midnight in the Garden of Good and Evil*	Clint Eastwood	–	Producer
1999	*True Crime*	Clint Eastwood	Steve Everett	Producer
2000	*Space Cowboys*	Clint Eastwood	Dr. Frank Corvin	Producer, composer
2002	*Blood Work*	Clint Eastwood	Terry McCaleb	Producer
2003	*Mystic River*	Clint Eastwood	–	Producer, composer
2003	*A Decade Under the Influence*	Richard LaGravenese	Himself	–
2004	*Million Dollar Baby*	Clint Eastwood	Frankie Dunn	Producer, composer
2006	*Flags of Our Fathers*	Clint Eastwood	–	Producer, composer
2006	*Letters from Iwo Jima*	Clint Eastwood	–	Producer
2007	*Grace is Gone*	James C. Strouse	–	Composer
2008	*The Changeling*	Clint Eastwood	–	–

First published in the United States in 2008 by Chronicle Books LLC.
First published in France in 2007 by Verlhac Editions.

Copyright © 2007 by Verlhac Editions.
"The Shy Kid from Oakland" copyright © 2008 by Peter Bogdanovic.
English translation copyright © 2008 by Chronicle Books LLC.

Library of Congress Cataloging-in-Publication Data available.

ISBN: 978-0-8118-6154-0

Manufactured in China

Translated and typeset by A-P-E Int'l

10 9 8 7 6 5 4 3 2 1

Chronicle Books LLC
680 Second Street
San Francisco, CA 94107

www.chroniclebooks.com

PHOTO CREDITS

13 | Eyedea
14 | Getty Images
15 | Associated Press / Sipa Press
16 | MPTV
19 | Getty Images
20 | Eyedea
21 | Sipa Press
22 | MPTV
23 | Getty Images
24 | Eyedea
25 | Sipa Press
26 | MPTV
27 | MPTV
29 | Hulton Archive / Getty Images
30 | Eyedea
31 | MPTV
32 | MPTV
33 | MPTV
34 | Sipa Press
35 | Eyedea
37 | Roger-Viollet
38 | MPTV
39 | MPTV
40 | MPTV
41 | MPTV
42 | MPTV
43 | Ullstein / Roger-Viollet
44 | Sipa Press
46 | Ullstein / Roger-Viollet
47 | Roger-Viollet
48 | Eyedea
49 | Corbis
50 | MPTV
51 | David Hurn / Magnum Photos
53 | Ullstein / Roger-Viollet
54 | MPTV
55 | MPTV
56 | Eyedea
57 | Corbis
58 | Eyedea
60 | MPTV
61 | Corbis
62 | Ullstein / Roger-Viollet
63 | Ullstein / Roger-Viollet
65 | Eyedea
66 | Eyedea
67 | MPTV
68 | MPTV
69 | MPTV
70 | MPTV

71 | Eyedea
72 | MPTV
73 | MPTV
74 | MPTV
76 | MPTV
77 | MPTV
79 | Ullstein / Roger-Viollet
80 | Eyedea
81 | Roger-Viollet
82 | Philip Halsman / Magnum Photos
83 | Philip Halsman / Magnum Photos
85 | MPTV
86 | MPTV
87 | MPTV
88 | Sipa Press
89 | Sipa Press
90 | Eyedea
91 | Eyedea
92 | Eyedea
93 | Roger-Viollet
94 | MPTV
95 | MPTV
96 | Roger-Viollet
97 | MPTV
98 | Ullstein / Roger-Viollet
99 | Ullstein / Roger-Viollet
100 | Eyedea
101 | Roger-Viollet
103 | Sipa Press
104 | Roger-Viollet
105 | Corbis
106 | Eyedea
107 | Roger-Viollet
108 | Corbis
110 | Corbis
111 | Corbis
112 | Sipa Press
114 | Gilles Peress / Magnum Photos
116 | Eyedea
117 | Eyedea
118 | Topfoto / Roger-Viollet
119 | Ullstein / Roger-Viollet
120 | Corbis
121 | Corbis
123 | Associated Press / Sipa Press
124 | Sipa Press
125 | Sipa Press
126 | Ullstein / Roger-Viollet
127 | Sipa Press
129 | Ullstein / Roger-Viollet

130 | Sipa Press
131 | Sipa Press
133 | Corbis
134 | Corbis
135 | Ullstein / Roger-Viollet
136 | Ullstein / Roger-Viollet
138 | MPTV
139 | Roger-Viollet
140 | Gueorgui Pinkhassov / Magnum Photos
143 | Corbis
145 | Associated Press / Sipa Press
147 | Ullstein / Roger-Viollet
148 | Roger-Viollet
149 | Roger-Viollet
151 | Associated Press / Sipa Press
152 | Corbis
153 | Roger-Viollet
154 | Associated Press / Sipa Press
155 | Associated Press / Sipa Press
156 | Corbis
158 | Sipa Press
159 | Corbis
161 | Eyedea
162 | Associated Press / Sipa Press
163 | Corbis
164 | Corbis
165 | Corbis
166 | Eyedea
167 | Eyedea
168 | Ullstein / Roger-Viollet
169 | Roger-Viollet
171 | Corbis
172 | Ullstein / Roger-Viollet
173 | Ullstein / Roger-Viollet
174 | Ullstein / Roger-Viollet
175 | MPTV
176 | Corbis
177 | MPTV
178 | Associated Press / Sipa Press
181 | Eyedea
182 | Associated Press / Sipa Press
183 | Associated Press / Sipa Press
185 | Associated Press / Sipa Press
186 | Associated Press / Sipa Press
187 | Associated Press / Sipa Press
188 | Corbis
189 | Corbis

Every effort has been made to trace the ownership of all copyrighted material included in this volume. Any errors that may have occurred are inadvertent and will be corrected in subsequent editions, provided that notification is sent to the publisher.